I0159820

ELEPHANTS (FRAGILE)

DAVID GILBERT

CinnamonPress

INDEPENDENT INNOVATIVE INTERNATIONAL

Published by Cinnamon Press
Meirion House
Tanygrisiau
Blaenau Ffestiniog
Gwynedd
LL41 3SU
www.cinnamonpress.com

The right of David Gilbert to be identified as author of this work has been asserted by him in accordance with the Copyright, Designs and Patent Act, 1988. Copyright © 2018 David Gilbert.
ISBN: 978-1-910836-94-1
British Library Cataloguing in Publication Data. A CIP record for this book can be obtained from the British Library.

All rights reserved. No part of this publication may be reproduced, stored in a retrieval system, or transmitted in any form or by any means, electronic, mechanical, photocopying, recording or otherwise without the prior written permission of the publishers. This book may not be lent, hired out, resold or otherwise disposed of by way of trade in any form of binding or cover other than that in which it is published, without the prior consent of the publishers.

Designed and typeset in Palatino by Cinnamon Press.
Cover design by Jan Fortune.
Printed in Poland
Cinnamon Press is represented in the UK by Inpress Ltd and in Wales by the Welsh Books Council

Contents

Elephants (Fragile)

She Said

That cut will take time to heal
You think too much
Double-bow your laces
Don't waste food—finish what's on your plate
Coffee doesn't taste as good as it smells
Double lock the door when we go out
Lock it at night when we stay in
Pay attention
German is not a nice language
Keep your head down—don't get involved
Not too much salt on that
Love is not like Hollywood
Try your best, but don't get your hopes up
Open the window at night to get some fresh air
The doctor may need to take your tonsils out
Heaven is a sensible idea—for some
A quiet life is a good life
No, I'm fine
Rules are there for a reason
I can tell when it will rain
I've never believed in a loving God
Imagine every other driver is an idiot
Be back before its dark
Don't speak too loudly in public places
There's no point talking about the past
You ask too many questions
Stay away from dogs—particularly Alsatians
Knife and fork together when done

Field Trip

On the botany field trip to Abergavenny
we paired up to investigate the flora
of an old cemetery with yellow lichen

spilling greedily over the grave stones
obliterating names of husbands and wives.
(Remember, they are half fungi, half algae,

living in symbiosis. They love the south.
Healthy growth is a sign of unpolluted air).
We threw quadrats into the long grass.

I like to imagine that I still could name
each specimen we found. But can't.
This was the morning of that famous last night

we got drunk with girls from another school
never to be seen again, holding hands
as long as we could in the dark.

The Best Christmas I Ever Had

The best Christmas I ever had
I made vegetable samosas
and carried them over to Paul's house
in an old ruck sack.

These are good, he said.
We cracked open a couple of cans
and talked a load of bollocks
for a couple of hours.

Then we got on our bikes
and sped across the city's empty streets,
not a sound above our breath
and brakes and wheels.

We stopped at a worker's café
for sugary tea and chocolate biscuits
then rode home to watch TV.
I was 22.

The World is Full of Toilets to Cry In

Old smelly ones of course, uninspected, with cracked floor tiles, damp inglorious seats and broken locks, where one tap gushes forever hot and the dryer doesn't work, even if you bang it several times. And where you're not so poorly as to fail to notice the plethora of metaphors.

I can feel more at home in posh ones, conference centres, government agencies and four star hotels (you can sometimes sneak in if you're desperate) where Mozart streams in from unidentifiable wall speakers and the soap and incense sticks, in your justifiable fury, are easily nicked.

There was one (after she left me) where the urinals were ringed in ultraviolet light like the one in Captain Scarlet and the Mysterons (though maybe that was white). It could be some sort of futuristic antiseptic. But it had me so captivated that I forgot. For a while.

But mostly I prefer the everyday ones, in railway stations or shopping centres, just about clean enough mostly, to let you know you're alright in the end, not too shiny to make you feel awkward for feeling so rubbish. And at least you're never alone. I don't mind paying 20p for one of those.

The Estuary

By the time the mist lifts above the estuary
it is a clear zero degrees by my reckoning—
hard fact like a cold nada.

The woman in the yellow mac has long since gone,
tilted boats are dug into the gluey mud
and a curlew sifts for stranded crabs.

My mum said that feelings come and go
that nobody has a monopoly on truth
and to bear the moon sick tides with equanimity

like a horse at the edge of a stubbled field
facing away from the wind,
but did not tell me what to do

with territories of emptiness
my wellies stuck in the shallow ooze
and red elements simmering in the gut.

The Cats (Morning in Madeira)

From the balcony before the heat of the day, of the day when things will start to crack, I watch the skinny feral cats collect on the high brick walls, the walls around the building site. This morning there are three kittens, three we've never seen, two ginger, one black, the black one nudging its dozing mum to wake, look up, look up to where the woman at the window will eventually throw down a few crusts of bread, a few down, and if they're lucky some scraps of meat. Way out at sea, a lone yacht bobs and tacks, and as it does, a cruise ship cuts across, scarlet and white and crawls, crawls into port and spins slowly around to display a vast woman's face, with one winking eye on its prow, then floats backwards towards land, engine low and growling. I can just make out a line of tiny passengers on the deck, the deck on which some are waving. I don't wave back. I seldom wave. Then two of them, the early workers' shift, arrive for their pre-eight o'clock cigarette. They sit on upturned buckets at right angles to each other, not looking at each other, one has a hat, then lean down, lean down and pick up their hammers. One day there'll be a swimming pool and this derelict house, the house with half-demolished walls, gutted rooms and skeletal roof will entertain millionaires we will never know. One picks up a stone, one stone from the pile on his right, turns it and examines it, the other does the same, then simultaneously they bring their hammers down and then the splinters are let loose, let loose and are flying from them, from the centre of the building site, from their blows and the woman closes her window, from their blows, and there's a scattering and the sending up of small explosions of dust from the soil, and after ten strikes or so, hard strikes, definite strikes, they lay the remaining core blown stone on top of a pile on the left, the pile that will slowly rise and rise and by the time I come struck back will have become a small empire of little rocks—a hill. They are never late. They never do more than ten minutes at a time before they rest and reach for another cigarette. They never seem to talk. I calculate they might smoke eighty cigarettes each by dusk. Their chip-chip-chip would have us mad. I wake the kids and we troop down to the café, the café with custard tarts, for the first of god knows how many cappuccinos. The heat is coming, the day already long and the cats, the cats have gone.

12

The Last of the Lighthouse Keepers

The last of the lighthouse-keepers
lifts the key one final time
to the door of his blackened home

descends the steep, cracked steps
locks down the stony monument
and rows across the bay.

That night, from the cliff top
the ocean spread at his feet
he summons the clouds to twist a storm.

The dark captain of the lost boat
unsighted, ungovernable
caught in the grip of the straits

lifts his face one final time
to the looming unlit tower
before ripping against the rocks.

Stevo — Legend

Rob's a right joker, arrives looking like he's had a really rough night, reckons he's up for a steady set of light weights. But under his breath, as he's getting undressed, he admits he's ready to puke. I give him stick about Saturday's results. He knows I'm just having a laugh, I think.

Dazza comes in — not sure where I am with him. Some of the lads reckon he gets a bit uptight if he comes in for too much stick. So, I'm just like *alright* and he reels off a story about one of his birds who's giving him jip and I'm agreeing they're all *more trouble than they're worth.*

Jonny's next in with a smirk and a shuffle and we hang five and do fists. He's alright is old Jonny. Never sure what he's up to though. Bit of a dark horse. Dazza says he's rock solid, decent landscape gardener and all round painter-decorator if you need something done for cash in hand.

Tommo's always been a bit of a plonker but he can be a right laugh. I remember the time he whipped some guys arse, went a little bit mental over a bottle of aftershave, stolen, so he said, while he'd been in the shower. Poor guy never came back: *how's it hanging Tommo?* I laugh from the lockers.

Stevo. Legend. Always in at 7, building up a six pack. Looks himself up and down in the mirror naked all the bloody time. We rib him a bit about that, but deep down we all wish it was us. And who doesn't give it a glance? Pull the old stomach in — can't be too harsh.

Vince has problems we don't talk about too much. Something to do with his dad who's seriously ill. Maybe dying. We only know 'cos the girl at reception is one gossipy cow. To look at him though you'd never know and I'm not sure I should ask. I give him a nod.

14

Jez. Blinder, true mate. Find myself waiting for his texts whenever I'm bored at work. Creases me up. But yesterday he didn't get in touch. And I'm like wondering where he's got to now—he's never this late—or if he really rates me. Suddenly

My head's a bit of a mess and I'm feeling bad like I'm some sort of girl. Worried. Pissed off. I'll do an extra set of weights to save me going nuts, 'cos I hate this. Hate this sort of... sort of feeling of not knowing where I stand with one of the lads.

The Jab

I slid between rooms
Severing wires

Unscrewing bulbs
And scissoring magazines

Limbs became heavier
And heavier to operate

I sat cross-legged
Fending off evil

While the bedroom wall
Grew dangerously thin

The black house began
Its whispering plots

My brother was sent
With poisoned Jaffa Cakes

Then came the scraping
And bleeding sound

Of thousands of chairs
Falling over themselves

Midnight's rush
Of telephone calls

Rose wailing and wolf-like
Four men arrived

Serious and muscular
The quiet jab came

And my mother's voice:
Please look after him

In the Name of Sound

When small, the boy was gentle
and held his hands over his ears at loud noise—

hand dryers in public toilets
the school trip to the fire station,
church bells and football crowds.

He cried when they shouted at him.

How could we know he had a sensitive brain?
That he was picking up aliens on galactic frequencies.

Now he is Chief Listener
to the callings of the Universe
and in his spare time
eavesdrops on troubled beings.

He tells us of a wilderness
where scarlet poisonous berries grow in neglected fields
and nearby, of a whole nation, woolly and wild
that lunges and yells.

His face turns sad: *They have forgotten*
how to be alone in their rooms,
or with each other—
all in the name of sound.

Nuthouse Marriage

Nurse Evelina dubbed it
The Nuthouse Marriage.

Wedded with sacred string.

But even Father Adrian
was adrift
as he twinned our fingers
and spied our wrists.

Kevin, in a warm car, pretending
it was part of occupational therapy,
drove us to the park
to hold hands on a cold bench for half an hour.

We kissed hugely before the bays
divided us at night.

And in the morning, you wore a pale pink hat—
You were against strong colours.
You vowed: *I will ride my way*

out of here on a broom.
Who was I
to argue?

We listened to The Mission.
We locked the laundry room from inside

rehearsed across the rain
to outwit
the spun coin—the loneliness

of ill-fortune, mechanics of the universe
and cackles
behind the observation window

or the well-meaning prayers
of the forgetful.

Close Obs

I'm curled into a ball
on a thin mattress on the floor
covered with a crinkly nylon sheet
smelling faintly of sick and piss.

Outside the heavy brown door
sits Len, muscly, tanned,
with *The Mirror* crossword.
Not much older than me,

he's done his fair share
of hurtling down corridors
readying needles full of Depixol
to slam into the arses of lunatics

like me I suppose.
As my sobbing slows
I hear him humming tunelessly
and clicking the end of his pen:

Mate, your mum said
you didn't use to be such a dickhead.
Let's see. Try this for starters:
French for dead-end, 3-2-3?

The Bear of Suicide

How else to deal with the aforementioned bear in the wardrobe?
He is still cross
and wants out.

To tie him up again would be another ordeal
and I am short of ammunition.
But hang on, stupid me, he isn't shootable.
Why is that funny?

It was all I could do yesterday to keep him
preoccupied with stale biscuits
while I went to the bathroom.

By the time I got back, he was a mealy mouthed prophet
who declared war on my way of tackling the doubt.
Can a bear do that?

And his mouth was drooling.
Was he rabid?
Was he more dangerous dead than alive?
Would he haunt me?
Oh dear sweet Bear God, these questions!

What did he want for breakfast?
I decided to change again
but yellow is not my colour.
And this seemed to make him more irritable.
How so?

I was once flattered that he had fallen for a human
and such an ordinary quizzical soul.
But then I thought, blimey, what is it with us
that we think that bears even care?

He is in my air zone—I can feel his meaty breath.
He has always said I should get used to his presence.
Is he cousin to the Grizzly last Summer? Sorry
I get confused with sub-categories.

He is strangling me first, I think.
There is a rope, yes.
He is a blur of bear and taking himself
into my deeper consciousness.
Drowning might have been easier.

But since when have I had a choice
over living, let alone dying?

The Builder

The builder is busy with his treachery
leaning this way and that into ladders

fetching strange tools and materials
from his beat up van. He desires

my ageing walls. This business
of cleansing and repair an excuse

to claw at tiles and devour rooves
without doubt, without anger.

I have felt this day coming since we moved in.
He is up there, wondering about, light footed

as if he owned the place—the palace of air—
like the crows every 7am.

I don't know the technicalities—he has me
in the maw of his expertise.

When done, he will peer at the innards—
our soft furnishings, my carpet tracks—

and tomorrow corral his mates,
the timid but ruthless scavengers.

I must admit I am meat and half
in love with the power of this inevitable stranger

bold as the exposed crossbeams
perilously high, unblinking in the wind

sun up soft on his sweated back
silhouetted against the opening sky,

staring down through me
cowering in my wait for new skin.

Ceasefire

There is a trembling in the woods.
A machine gun.

The woodpecker's bass drill.
Thinking of how its neck muscles, thickened skull and third inner eyelid

prevent damage to the brain.
I am with my father again

in the clearing by the Red Arches.
I take off my glove, and finger the burning cold

hold out my hand in the only way I can—a peace gesture.
He tells me to stay very still

and all I know is uneasy and my body frozen
like listening for glass

or an eye above watching me.
The way a nuthatch returns—

me trailing its flight—
dipping in a long low u from the highest of trees

takes me from awareness of breathing
and the stomach drops

and its small black eye aims at the hand
and its black beak at the seed in my hand.

Over and over again
I must stand here in the trembling woods

for the attack
and ceasefire.

Elephants (Fragile)

Not yet. You are not yet ready.
They are not yet ready for you.

This morning, the warm hold of the small room
Haydn's sweet piano through your ribs
making you think of playgrounds
and suddenly tears.

The white sun through the condensation on the glass.
The window jammed.

You waited in the silence.
The scary, crazy silence.
You tried to scare yourself with thought
and its drilling down
and when done for a while
you tried to scare yourself with silence.

Walk eyes down.
Eyes down.

The white painted cross on the pavement.
The builder who *fuck it, I left my fucking new phone at Screwfix.*
The 'First Class Garage'.

Last night, you read of the island in the Finnish archipelago
and the adventures of grandmother
lying down and watching the feather
loosen itself from the blade of grass.

This morning, you got ready slowly.
You wanted the words for a story of yourself:
Lightness. Tentativeness. Nothing quite expressed—
vulnerability not quite.
Resilience. Re-silence. You wish.

Then you remembered when you moved house.
Stacking the small wooden figures in little boxes marked:
Elephants (Fragile).

Bay of Ghosts

When she laughs
She looks down
Her lids flutter
And she closes her eyes

When she closes her eyes
She looks down
On a trail of white petals
And gathers her dress

Her lids flutter
And she is riding a horse
And when she rides
Her eyes are laughing

The wind rises
And when the wind rises
She hears the ghosts
And their fluttering laughter

When they laugh
She steps into a boat
For the Bay of Ghosts
And gulls beckon

The wind laughs
And the gulls look down
She closes her eyes
And her laugh is the gulls

And is the laughter
Of the island rising
And when the island rises
The laughter is the closing of eyes

And the Bay of Ghosts
Is petals and laughing
And fluttering and ghosts
And while she is away

When she is a ghost
And gone from us
Our eyes are wide open
And we look up

Our mornings flutter.
But she will come for us
We will gather like petals
When we are petals

We will close our eyes
When we close our eyes
and look down
Our eyes will flutter

We will laugh
And when we laugh
She will take us across
To the Bay of Ghosts

Back in Town

I would better recognise this place
if there were a dove
or some mad man broke from the cover of that hedge
and screamed hallelujah.

Failing that, a pigeon would do.
The weather is nailed grey
everything levelled out.

They've planted saplings by the rails,
the old church is surrounded by fork lift trucks
as if they're getting ready to up it into the sky.
And my favourite wine bar has gone.

Maybe I should not have come back.
I know that this is how it has to happen
like everyone with cancer must wake at 3am
alone at the alone time
the hours having moved before they were ready.

All stories of beautiful returns are lies.
They are uneventful
and rely on witnesses
you don't often see at this hour of the morning.

Take that man on the bench
as he sweeps his thumb across his screen.
Been out all night.
And even if he looked up,
wouldn't know me now from Adam.

He knows and I know
we may now be equal, but we are still restless
that what we recreate is as meaningless
as what we have dismantled.

I want to tell him love is glue. But
it looks like he will have to re-learn it
the hard way.

For now, the chances of such meetings
are hardly propitious.
And I need a good breakfast
before it all begins again.

The Baby Starling

When the church bells stopped
and the empty courtyard filled with birdsong
I thought of the baby starling without a tail
that had fluttered into the Italian restaurant

and startled the woman
who spilled minestrone onto her best dress
then threatened to send them the laundry bill
while her friends killed themselves laughing

and the way some children
born in towns, never get to the ocean
and how I could have taken mum
to Vienna one more time. And how

when everything turned out alright again,
you looked at me and said: *There, you see?*

Morden Via Bank

Fell asleep at Tufnell Park missed Camden Town went sailing via Charing Cross came up at Warren Street. *Well, what the hell,* I thought turned right, zigzagged unfamiliar streets walked into a foyer, took a lift to an office that sort of looked OK sat down at a desk, scanned the in-tray then got up to make a coffee. Don't think anyone noticed till lunchtime when a guy with blue eyes said: *Hey, Steve. You all right? You look kind of pale. Must have been a rough night.* A woman with glasses said: *Have you done something to your hair? Suits you.* Then she left me with papers to read and file. Drafted a couple of emails then realised I had a one o'clock meeting with the senior management team: *Nice tie* said the Chief Executive before we got down to business. *It's been a long day,* I thought later as I wrote an overdue Board paper on Exception Reporting. I hadn't even had lunch. It was already getting dark. I put my coat on, headed back to the station and wondered whether I'd get home too late or find another one.

As Ghost

As ghost, exhausted by my efforts,
I will dwell on the small things that I miss,
the rippling colours through the frosted glass
the spare tile leaning against the wall

patient, so as to be useful at last,
blotchy stains on the bathroom mirror,
the yellow mop and bucket clothed in dust
and grey sad soap stone elephant,

its trunk curling around itself, the slow
rumble of dutiful cars as darkness lifts
the regular assembly of restive crows
in the bare trees, the way light rolls

across the air in loving waves to reach
out for the retina —
and you asleep —
and if touch
hadn't been taken from me by then
I would do more with less, would kiss you more.

The Man from Autoglass

I take a cup of coffee—milk no sugar—
out to the man from Autoglass.
The windscreen is chipped at the top
in the shape of a low hung u
not yet blocking my view of the roads sufficiently
for the car to fail its MOT
but bad enough to call the insurance bods—
90 quid seemed reasonable. I offer
chocolate digestives but he says he's put on
so much weight over Christmas
that his wife would tell him off.
I have locked myself out. The well-fed fox
at the edge of the park opposite
pauses. The bins are overflowing. The rain
turns steady, the morning dark and directionless
I notice, despite myself,
the smell of coffee, petrol and wet grass.

Once, an Avocet

I used to be able to sit
on a rough wooden bench
in a hide on the north-eastern point of the Norfolk Broads
with jam sandwiches
and big binoculars
and big brother in his grown up kagool
in my knitted light blue jumper with a wide white hoop
waiting for the waders
to come sift the marsh at low tide
water still sloshing in my wellies
and the tatty grubby print tacked onto the gnarled wall
depicting knot, sanderling, curlew, oyster catcher
the wind throbbing over the corrugated iron roof
thinking about what would be on telly
dying to itch my bum
heroically still for nature's sake
because, beyond anything and football
I wanted to be Bellamy or Attenborough.
Was it worth it? It was cold.
Sometimes we saw the usual
muddy greys and browns
red legs, yellow legs, tall, squat, long billed, short, slow and the quick,
once, an avocet
which we ticked off in *The Observer Book of Birds*
the marvel of a flock lifting simultaneously against the dying sun.
Mostly it was tedious as hell
particularly when we had finished the cheese and onion crisps
that we melted on the tongue so as not to crunch.
But I used to be able to sit.

To be the rain

slipping from the cold
grip of the sea
discrete, almost invisible
drawn by the heat

gathered into the hold
and urgency
of the tightening cloud
and its atmospheric thrust

then departing again, hurled
as indivisible sheets
through flights of birds

released, unfurled
enveloping earth
like a lover returned

www.ingramcontent.com/pod-product-compliance
Lightning Source LLC
Chambersburg PA
CBHW032115040426
42337CB00041B/1432